Parts of Speech

PARTS OF SPEECH

KYLE SCHLESINGER

CHAX PRESS / 2014

ISBN: 978-0-9894316-9-9

Grateful acknowledgment to the editors and publishers of the magazines in which some of the poems in this book first appeared: *5 Trope; 6x6; Brooklyn Rail; Cannibal; Colorado Review; Damn the Caesars; Do You Believe?; Drill; Eaogh; Inter; Matchbook; Muthafucka; Name; No, Dear; The Offending Adam; Peaches & Bats; Rave On; Satellite Telephone; Spiral Orb; Try!; Turntable Blue Light;* and *With + Stand.* Additional thanks to the publishers of the chapbooks in which these poems appeared: *Bad Words to the Radio & Other Poems* (Least Weasel Press, 2011); *Business Casual* (No Press, 2011); *Commonplace* (Cuneiform Press, 2011); *Dark Glasses* (No Press, 2010); *Look* (No Press, 2008); *Picture Day* (Electio Editions, 2012); *The Pink* (Kenning Editions, 2008); *Squarely* (housepress, 2004); and *What You Will* (NewLights Press, 2011). "Loose Ends" is a collaboration with filmmaker Scott Stark that premiered online at *OnAndOnScreen* in conjunction with *Bomb Magazine* in 2011, and "Goes Without Saying" was published as a limited-edition broadside by Eucalyptus Press in 2010.

for Ted

Everybody knows that art is made by
inspiration, but they still prop it up.
— Agnes Martin

This thinking is wrong, I know.
— Lucia Berlin

It was there, but now you are contained
in a thing already changing, bring-
ing you into its terms—and your house
shrinks, far off, and things are bright
and twisted.
— Robert Creeley

CONTENTS

I

Dark Glasses	13
Loose Ends	22
Picture	23
First Person	24
As If	25
Awol	26
Coast	27
Goes Without Saying	28
Whenever	29
Smooth Sailing	30
Calypso	31
Don't Be Aloud	32
Big Deal	33
Let It Rest	34
Better Ask	35
Business Casual	36
Bad Words to the Radio	37
Dream	48

II

Commonplace	51
What You Will	65
The Long Goodbye	67
Today	68
Lost Wall	69
I'm Always Being	70
Just a Thought	71
There's Nothing More	72
When the Shit Hits the Fan	73
Stringing Bobbles	74
Stands to Reason	75
Groove With	79
Casa de Lava	80
Diagonals Always	81
Aren't We Always	82
To the Letter	83

III

You Won't Believe It	91
Look	100
Suite Sixteen	109
Shabbat Saloon	110
Hey Nancy	111
Shedding	113
Liner Notes	117
Or Say a Mark	119
Squarely	121
Treatise	122
Carnation	124
Picture Day	125
Just Passing Through	131

I

DARK GLASSES

From a grove of
Coconut palms
What seemed to be

Squinted down
Afternoon haze
Insert a trace

Into the gesture
You know what
You are when it's

Over monkey grass
Across clearing
Like a robin

Paused to gaze
A dozen seconds
Stumbled across

What was an
Epiphany of sorts
Went on eyes

Wandered ask
Questions say
Something only

Thing that came
To mind
You know

You know like
Where's here
Turned back to

Door slice of
Infinity which
Was seldom

Cruising taxi
Long gone
There were

Others but
Once a little
High a few

New lines in
Sand so brown
So they bounced

Isn't it curious
Put the prefix in
And do what's

What happened
In the hills when
Historical parallels

Yeah, they're useful
So's television
Squirreled away

In a headline
High lama
Sacred flame

Think of that
And for what
Crosshatch patterns

Turned selves in
An old elm
Across the street

Heard footsteps
Behind the door
But the door

Didn't open
Not impossible
Beneath the wavy

Blond behind
Puzzled puppy
Uncanny shrug

Not exactly
A sole source
Not altogether

Kiss in the foyer
Slice of lemon
Read directions

Mesmerized
That's understood
Another given

You know
Come on upstairs
Wait for water

Decide what to drive
Light a cigarette
Put face to name

Back to table
Fold lengthwise
Into fourths

Sign on shirtboard
Weight stayed lost
Stopped to turn

Retraced steps
Twitch waltz
Hard to miss

No hurry
On the level
Of the garage

Across the street
Behind the wheel
Old coot

Tie the toe
Tags on make sure
Yen for cupcakes

In the saddle
To the stars
Clicked into place

Shades of blue
View from house
Back to ocean

Only something
Everybody's somebody
Now what

What else
This and that
Looking around

Crimp a little
So what happened
Couple of times

No maybe about
Whatever turned up
Somebody don't

Know exactly who
Down from hills
After the sniff

So it would seem
An interesting notion
Kind of split

Frown went way
Grin came back
Split three ways

Which isn't bad
Not good
But not bad

Money's money
On the floor
Which is more

For the most part
A windowless room
On the bedroom

Room's more interesting
Way to keep score
Maybe but didn't

That's the point
Didn't wrinkle
So riddle this

Behind which
Laughter bubbled
With ice in it

Out of past
Seersucker shorts
Breakfast buffet

Find out what happened
Spruce up a little
People like to forget

One last look
Late lunch
Who hovered

Last stop
Look at that
Cold snap

Wrong turn
Into gridlock
Almost dark

Red X rush of
Cold around door
Into room

Just like that
No socks no
Shoes nothing

What or who
List goes on
Not really

White money
Slipped it on
Nothing moved

At dinner last night
Should've asked
To grease skids

Cross a few palms
Above the chin
With skin

What now
Patted the bed
Traffic was light

On the curves
Because riding
In the back

Worth the wait
Paint was faded
Behind dark glasses

LOOSE ENDS

A kind of fog rolls
Souls' aglow in pinup
Patterns from the horse's
Lines edges and planes

Someplace in the desert
I know well where I'll go
Nuts just waiting there
Funny synopsis oblique

Banter live air in a pinch
Some call it emotional
On the other hand
There's the other hand

Dishing out pad thai
Minnows spoon
In a matchbox where
The line begins again

PICTURE

standing
next
to
you

FIRST PERSON

for Anna

Cronies love hoodies
Vicodin blue afternoon
Televised suffice to
Say you know tomorrow's
Gonna be another day
Mishap with friends
Like that the riot act
Tangerine dream just
Kidding this shit's
Amazing beg to differ
Be the wiser soul
Searching sounds fishy
Wish me well until we
Meet again send my
Regards to yesterday's
News like nobody's
Business that aside
Six of one so many
Words all in your head

AS IF

here
I
am

AWOL

for Brenda

Hip tease straight to
Uppercut who gets
Placebo heady times
Bona fide chops all
Bets are off smack
Dab in proportion
To human interest
Story whoop whoop
Grand ol' Marxist days
Laurels befall tenure
History you can write
In bright green crayon
But you can't own
Language someone you
Thought you knew
Brings you back to the
Stats doesn't every
Body look great
Everyone parties
Little throb old flame

COAST

goes
and
goes
and
goes

GOES WITHOUT SAYING

for Michael

Split infinitive goes
Without saying what's
A synonym for COD how
Many riddles have you
Squirreled away the
Road to hell is paved
With permanent marker
Blacking out as night
Moves in or have you
Seen a feeling for
Leaving track without
Trace or didn't you
Come along for ride
Dog eat dog picture
Perfect perfect picture
Anything you do every
Thing you are take it
Or where do I sign
Double click one room
Over sparked déjà vu

WHENEVER

you
feel
like
it

SMOOTH SAILING

for Bill

Tires hiss on blacktop
Line continues to the
Point where muscles
Become fatigued the
Breath exhausted just
Then glimmers rally
Sideways an unusually
Attractive replica in
Threadbare barbershop
Just for the fun of it
Ask me anything you're
All existentialists
Loosing equilibrium
Going down after it in
What you might call
A relative wilderness
Looking at credentials
The form of a question
Common denominator
Running numbers in the
Haze of a shoeshine

CALYPSO

better
go
see

DON'T BE ALOUD

for Stacy

You know the story is
Generally lavender
Start over skip to
Scrimmage go figure
Feeling starts with
Black ribs lock arms
At a loss for words
Trip you up continues
Strike through cut to
Second person singular
Number one what else
Is there facts of life
A screwy sensation
Sets in what begets
Beg to differ cinnamon
Soap you dig dodge
Hold it in thinking of
Stand and deliver hi
I'd like that you could
Clear some doubts that
I have something's up

BIG DEAL

only
to
me

LET IT REST

for Rich

Spooky foxes seem
Alright meaning the
Message is ajar trance
Doesn't do it live
Like possible question
Intuits other habits
Crave snug gaze in a
Relative clause where
Irony seats itself
What difference does
It can count on thing
Of the past under the
Bridge to beg your
Pardon FYI just the
Two of us last to know
You know who's to say
What's happening and
What's not at your own
Risk like it is up to
Here keep the change
Eight days a week

BETTER ASK

for
another

BUSINESS CASUAL

Everyone stands around
Asking which way they
Went was the car black
Or brown was the top

Up or down afternoon
Aglow twilight returns
With a twist what goes
Around I know a Judy

Mechanical arm reaches
For the cigarette
Machine clearing the
Room so what's love

Got to do with it
What's a euphemism
For forever GOP or
Get off the pot

BAD WORDS TO THE RADIO

Lil iffy
Canned history
With a
Gizzi twist
Certain hunch
Hypnotic grunge
Get the gist
Magic fingers

Take the shape
So much
Hubbub glitters
Black tie only
Dry cleans
Night beams
Battleship down
Acme speech

Code bitty
Loafer zip
When appropriate
Notch add
You glad
I am too

Be somebody
See something

Help me find
Flux neon
Skinny dip
Grass roots
Light dims
How much
Sentences inch
Trail goes

Cold ad
Nauseum
Whathaveyou
Cobbled together
Who's left
Who's right
I'm what
You might

Call whose
To say
Question
Assertion
Past tense
Eyes present

Or maybe
I'm seeing

Things out
The window
Water lurks
Facts muddy
Wait on
This weight
On the old
Switcheroo

Edge all you
Can spiel
Reading ghost
Obit automation
Pompom in
The palm
Of my
Griddle way

Moon glimpse
Next suffix
Sure fire
Feed loop
Yellow sunglasses
Luke warm

Idea no
Rush hour

Flies nowhere
Cottage old
Adage see
For your
Self what's
That tuna
Salad what's
That tuna

Salad hold
Everything let
Loose with
All you've
Got getting
On getting off
Experience the
Taste you're

Always last
To know who
Knew so what
Sorta fluffy
Puppy nudge
Wanna know

Never thought
Of this as

A thought
Presto change-o
People live
Like that
Reiterate more
Or less the less
I think the
Breezier it gets

Questions facts
Face in hard
Daylight at a
Stand still I
Focus on
Spots comma up
For anything
Gets me

Ass backwards
Nuts at
Peace with
The world
Pierced sanctity
Beg your

Come again
Certain Sundays

Off the cuff
So far from
Home first
Word number
Two something
Hobnobbing
With washed
Up terrorists

Somebody said
Didn't know
About something
Somebody said
Having a good
Time iffy
Situation long
Vacation long

Division something's
Missing in my
Anybody I
You'll be
The first a
Little place

Pant pant
Highway robbery

Frumpy jumper
Big car cronies
Something to
Spare for
Things were
Winding down
It's not
A hallucination

When listen
Something changes
And don't
Know who
Moves
So fast
Then the
Lights go

Out and
Never come
Don't let
The door
Takes time
Direct address

You have
To keep

Moving down
And back
Up and
Down the
Window fits
The frame
Smile becomes
Simile canaries

The knob
Makes knees
Heart to
Headphones
Somewhere in
Derry at the
Wheel moving
Along take

Advantage
The air
Really clean
One step
At a what
You don't can't

Be the wiser
Broken headlights

Speed of sound
See self blink
Doozy must
The girl
Stumped
Bruiser bone
Crusher funny
Coincidence I've

Been asking
Timely manner
Orderly fashion
Shifty numbers
Ah-ha four letter
Words don't
Come cheap
Checkered history

Marks the
Spot with
A gun
In an
Airport time
Flies when

You're having
Noodle around

Record skips
See what
Sticks remember
Browse all
Day nothing
To write
Home about
If the

Shoe fits
Bad words
To the
Radio
A certain
Someone a
Pot to
Piss in

A life
To live
You're perceptive
You just
Don't see
It yet

Things are Looking up

DREAM

You know that
Feeling you get
The night before
A pet dies

That's exactly the
Way I feel before
The word appears
In the white rectangle

II

COMMONPLACE

for Scott

Birds in a net
Swish
Through a cloud

Tubes cross
Patterns patterns
Patterns

Not a word
Of it to any
One

Overhead
Trains cross
Almost forgot

Ancient ashtrays
On a wing
One more thing

Sign rolls up
Sign rolls down
Train rolls

Round the bend
Ratchet it up
In and out

Like that
Hours mirror
Hours

Keep passing
Window blink
Bon voyage

Everything moves
At a clip
Brink purple

Church nest
Sheep all
The things

We do
All day
All things

You can't play
By yourself
Body breath

Spare time
Time spares
In a field

Music improves
Bell weather
With others

What's love
Got to do
Got to do

The hardest thing
Is finding a way
To talk about it

Not saying
Distance spaces
Space for

The reader
Word disappears
World comes back

Speechless
Almost oblique
Veil from face

To typeface
As difficult as
Keeping an

Appointment
With an erasure
A way of thinking

Not a style
Background
Two and four

Dancer dance
To this
If you

Something wonderful
May happen
Hands on

Hands off
Learning on
The job

Do not touch
Keep ball rolling
Conversation

Continues
On stone
No expectations

No spectators
Obligation builds
Art is serious

Enough already
There is no point
In taking it

Too seriously
Seriously
What they think

In common
Represented only
By what they do

Separately elegant
Pomp and circumstance
Why we do

What we do
Wouldn't you?
Get your own goat

Socialism in
Its smallest
Most personal form

I hope I wasn't too
Terrible I just wanted
Something to happen

Who you are
Through play
Who can build

The tallest tower
It will disappear
Without me

Cell is not cellular
Two blues
Pass by

Couples not twins
On a two wheeler
Built for three

A company
In the screen
Beyond the screen

Cut off by
The music
Consider the

Geometry
Which is
Centuries old

Older than
America a
Model of Rome

In the foyer
Linking logs
And frog legs

In real time
In real time
They won't be

Here forever
A little rain and
Loss of inhibition

Days get longer
Not stronger
Resistance is

Contingent
On the force of
The costume

That masks
Face the eyes
Are as I remember

The face
Eyes the
Same

Footprints a
Habit of
Recurrent change

Keep it
Participles pass
Particular fact

You're certain
You're certain
An echo of every

Color in shacks
And chutes and
Ladders

Look at the corners
Picture the picture
Without the frame

Picture the picture
Without knowing
The artist

What do you
Think you know
Canvas unrolls

Edges vanish
Into thin
And reseed

Into the corners
Cut off center
The white space

Impossible to fill
With words
Cut off center

The white space
Not so much a hub
But a location

Sirens continue
To wail wall to
Wall ceilings

I'm sprung
On all fours
Cut off center

Where the center
Can be heard in
Plain sight

Gates anchor
Can't call collect
In plain sight

Go figure
It's perfect
We have what

You might call
A situation
On our hands

Hands on
Hands off
Go figure

If I were a mystic
My father would say
My son the mystic

Presence is grace
Where is the
Generosity today?

It's not a gift
Just something I
Want you to have

Commissions and
Invitations cages
And gingerbread

Essay without
Margins a rolling
Pun the cut

Of the signature
Someplace like Africa
Inverted commas

Angles gone under
The truth in painting
But not the essays

General delivery
People on the move
Kept until someone

Comes to claim it
Laguardia place
2-4-6-8

You can't take it
With you your words
Not yours

Stay
Life is too short
Poetic art starts

With the puffing
Of the lips
Shoot from the

Boulevard
Hello there is more
To learn from the

Top of a letter
Than the bottom
We don't see the words

As forms
Interlocking lives
Hands off

Seventh Avenue
Well paid
The dive

And 'avenue' is
Such a weird word
On the surface

Stills shattered
Match the intensity
Of the line

But the opposite
Referring to what
He referred to

Playful but referential
Who owns the work
Why travel

On the bus to Ohio
On a boat to Italy
On a train to France

What do you think
When you work with
Yourself

In every sexual
Relationship there are
At least three people

Involved according
To Freud
The fold

Paper on paper
Other side
Engage the wall

A breath of air
On a piece of paper
Spray paint

I colored the paper
I'm not sure I really
Engaged with it as

A text
Free as a bird
Fast as it gets

WHAT YOU WILL

Then schism
Comes to mind
Caramel drones
Or so they say
Touch of this
Pinch of that
Shiite zones
Butterfly staples
Hard to stomach
Ifs ands but
Another center
Cuts fusion
Never forget
According to who
Sic puppy
To the syrupy
Section of your
Inter body
Ain't never
Inches sense
Tense that's
Whose either
Checkered history
An inner peace

Stet circa
Small wonder
Switches up
Curtains glade
Needles glide
Wave crossing
Talk this and
That throw it
In reverse

THE LONG GOODBYE

Lighter than a whisper
Whisper tighter than a
Tijuana cigarette

TODAY

I'm thinking
Of something else
Yesterday tomorrow
Somehow

I'm thinking
Blown chaos
Something else
Wait for now

Looks like
I'm walking

LOST WALL

I feel responsible
In my pajamas

I'll never ever
Wear pajamas again

I'M ALWAYS BEING

Split in half rip-
Ripe film patterns the
Conspiracy normalcy
How to get to bottom

Looked into smeiotics
Really like syntactics
It makes the least sense
I need a job but dont really

Want one I need inspiration
But my stomach keeps this
And why there and how my
Brain says shut up I say

To my brain and the
Whirlwind continues to
Get frozen I care but I
Cant be sure

Sorry for the lack of
Puntuation right now
I do not care Ifeel good
For 7 minutes today

JUST A THOUGHT

Whatever ideas
I used to have
About a counter
Culture got shot
A long time ago
Like in the sixties
Or something

THERE'S NOTHING MORE

To it
Than that

The sky is
Broken and

It's making
A mess

WHEN THE SHIT HITS THE FAN

When the shit hits the fan
It does so en masse
When the shit hits the fan
It does so
Button never works
Button never works
That girl over there
Looks like a friend
Looks like a friend
That girl looks like
Any computer
Any computer
Know where I'm going
Know where I'm going
Inch by inch
Row by row
Gonna make
This garden grow
Gonna make this
Furrow for sure

STRINGING BOBBLES

Maud collar

STANDS TO REASON

for Miles

Everything at once
Curlicues do you mind
Mixed company off
Colour humor
That's the ticket
One for the money
Speechified logic
Enter uncertainty

And become
Curlicues do you mind
Tacit turn spin
Convex conveyer
Curved word for words
Who knows DNA
Summery highlighting
Homage to David Carson

Sharp edges sigh
Ladder not quite leaning
Mixed company off
The cuff for the record
Pitched to the former
Forgive and forget

All or nothing
Slip into something

Nobody knows
Knock knocks aside
Shadows ELO
Colour humor
Welcome to the index
A book of signatures
Want names
Where ledgers walk

Pursuit of happiness
Abstracts I sleep
On a JZ factor
Sensation burns
That's the ticket
On the books
But that is of course
Only a picture

Let the date alone
The blind have no shame
Don't want information
Object a portion
Where beauty roads
One for the money

As far as that goes
Something sunk in

Resembles a facade
Notch notch who's
Subtexts aside how
Strange and
Finks resonate
Pure pedigree
Speechified logic
Everything must goes

Minute thrice
With dub amp
Funny (not ironic)
Smart (not clever)
One need only think
Of mimicry
Similarly
Enter uncertainty

Enter uncertainty
Speechified logic
One for the money
That's the ticket
Colour humor
Mixed company off

Curlicues do you mind
Everything at once

GROOVE WITH

A little longing goes along
Should but it ain't
They're still buzzing around
Like dreams sheaf skillet
Honeycomb
Your hair
Eye drops morons in
A morning crust
Ready to move
At the drop of a hat
You could hear a pin
Drop of rain drop
Your drawers and go
Back to the drawing board
Out of my skull
Doubled me double you
Dixie cup I'll drink you
Under the table
Before you hatch
Stone in my shoe

CASA DE LAVA

for Gregg

History is only
Skin deep
As family does
Pay your dues
And continue to
Happening between
You and me there is
Always an and
When you double-not
You ought to be
Streaking on mean streets

DIAGONALS ALWAYS

We've passed
If we can can a book a place,
Relentless linearity: one sign
[space after colon]
Refridgerator (sp)
Approachs (sp)
Even if it (for "it it")

AREN'T WE ALWAYS

Body part
And whole
What it is
Senses typing
The itch moves
Just enough to
Joke it laugh
Line could go
Fingers mind
Stink a little
Stand up
Out of habit

TO THE LETTER

Anticipation flight
Successful look
Shrewd sensitive

Tough businessmen
Dabble intelligence
Close afternoon

Upon feeling
Following conversation
Insults implied

Life indifference
Reactions involved
Residue roundtable

Such hatred
Artists would
Publicly focus

Please be
Pertinent defenses
Confuse waiting

Until willing
Escapes always
Public flower

From down
Think brawl
Should reject

Responsibility fine
Roll paper
Dig smear

Flunky would
Accidentally stumble
In OK

Picture gesture
Public will
Whole canvas

Blank fabric
From factory
Years would

Canvas that
Is wouldn't
Scholar clean

From proof
Work proven
Study oversimplify

This important
Preliminary knowledge
Second would

Interesting misinformed
Different contempt
Cross-section difference

Without qualities
Included reaction
Selection in

Off fully
On merit
Modernist without

Strictly gallery
Such selfish
Fashion fads

Reject insist
Direct glaze
In front

Disappeared long
Cool ago
Reaction always

Nearing fifty
Of work
Boredom take

Up questions
Assault ultimate
Earliest gist

Which lift
Social culture
Found cleanest

Most civilized
Indulged citizens
Intolerable handle

Mannequins next
Of lifelike
Position horror

Cruddy rapport
With living
Recall grisly

Welfare group
Wooden grin
Spells sphinxish

Knowing should
Paint life
Continue to

Architecture
Into amenities
Paradoxical smile

Unreticent couple
Girls for females
From eastern

Choice words
Finding needles
Still rails

III

YOU WON'T BELIEVE IT

Downtown approval
Closing time
Bad vibes
Downtown approval
Bad vibes
What you talkin' bout
Downtown approval
Closing time
What you talkin' bout
Over by the door
Can't believe it
What you talkin' bout
Can't believe it
Too much
What you talkin' bout
Over by the door
Too much
Speak what I feel
Everything okay now
Too much
Everything okay now
For you
Too much
Speak what I feel

For you
Telephone call
By the balls
For you
By the balls
Gotta go
For you
Telephone call
Gotta go
Love to you
You're alright
Gotta go
You're alright
Will ya
Gotta go
Love to you
Will ya
Shit that
How ya doin'
Will ya
How ya doin'
Hostage understand
Will ya
Shit that
Hostage understand
Got everything
When I'm being fucked

Hostage understand
When I'm being fucked
I like to get kissed a lot
Hostage understand
Got everything
I like to get kissed a lot
You got it
Use of language
I like to get kissed a lot
Use of language
Make it happen
I like to get kissed a lot
You got it
Make it happen
Coming back
Do it now
Make it happen
Do it now
Squeezed out
Make it happen
Coming back
Squeezed out
Day I knew him
What happened
Squeezed out
What happened
Son of a bitch

Squeezed out
Day I knew him
Son of a bitch
C'mon out
Bullshit
Son of a bitch
Bullshit
Trouble enough as is
Son of a bitch
C'mon out
Trouble enough as is
I'm a fuckin' star
Don't smoke
Trouble enough as is
Don't smoke
My body
Trouble enough as is
I'm a fuckin' star
My body
What for
Pays the rent
My body
Pays the rent
So confused
My body
What for
So confused

What sorta things
Yellows screamers
So confused
Yellows screamers
You name it
So confused
What sorta things
You name it
When things were going
So good
You name it
So good
I guess so
You name it
When things were going
I guess so
Don't wanna talk
Sheer exhibitionism
I guess so
Sheer exhibitionism
When you don't
I guess so
Don't wanna talk
When you don't
Need them
You know
When you don't

You know
That's it
When you don't
Need them
That's it
Everybody's alright
Have to see
That's it
Have to see
Don't look good
That's it
Everybody's alright
Don't look good
I figured
Sleep all the time
Don't look good
Sleep all the time
Something eh
Don't look good
I figured
Something eh
I'm dyin'
Listen to yourself
Something eh
Listen to yourself
Everybody needs money
Something eh

I'm dyin'
Everybody needs money
Nothin' on nobody
Really warped
Everybody needs money
Really warped
Better off
Everybody needs money
Nothin' on nobody
Better off
Giving up
Do me a favor
Better off
Do me a favor
Think I'm a part of it
Better off
Giving up
Think I'm a part of it
A snow job
Well look please
Think I'm part of it
Well look please
Nothing to do with it
Think I'm part of it
A snow job
Nothing to do with it
Yeah yeah

Supposed to say to you
Nothing to do with it
Supposed to say to you
Bon voyage
Nothing to do with it
Yeah yeah
Bon voyage
I didn't know you knew
Said a mouthful sweetheart
Bon voyage
Said a mouthful sweetheart
It's ridiculous
Bon voyage
I didn't know you knew
It's ridiculous
Everything
You know what love is
It's ridiculous
You know what love is
Out of the closet
It's ridiculous
Everything
Out of the closet
Into the streets
All the way
Out of the closet
All the way

Ten minutes
Out of the closet
Into the streets
Ten minutes
Sad moment
Things I said
Ten minutes
Things I said
Free of charge
Ten minutes
Sad moment
Free of charge
You wouldn't believe it

LOOK

Who got shot
Got shot
See ya then
Who got shot
See ya then
Gonna take that
Who got shot
Got shot
Gonna take that
I'll take it
Thing up to my mouth
Gonna take that
Thing up to my mouth
Worked you over
Gonna take that
I'll take it
Worked you over
Cup of coffee
Along for the ride
Worked you over
Along for the ride
Holdin' the bag
Worked you over
Cup of coffee

Holdin' the bag
Put you away
Kiddin' me
Holdin' the bag
Kiddin' me
Save yourself
Holdin' the bag
Put you away
Save yourself
How you doin'
How you doin'
Save yourself
How you doin'
How you doin'
Save yourself
How you doin'
How you doin'
Do me one favor
Not the heat
How you doin'
Not the heat
The humidity
How you doin'
Do me one favor
The humidity
Had a feelin'
You got it

The humidity
You got it
Next life
The humidity
Had a feelin'
Next life
Belly dancer
Goin' down
Next life
Goin' down
All bullshit about
Next life
Belly dancer
All bullshit about
Wanna ask you somethin'
Gotta be kiddin'
All bullshit about
Gotta be kiddin'
Asshole with dentures
All bullshit about
Wanna ask you somethin'
Asshole with dentures
One foot in shit already
Have to tell you
Asshole with dentures
Have to tell you
Want to tell you

Asshole with dentures
One foot in shit already
Want to tell you
Fuckin' brain in the head
The collar
Want to tell you
The collar
Disorienting effect
Want to tell you
Fuckin' brain in the head
Disorienting effect
Of the drug
Business to know people
Disorienting effect
Business to know people
Long way from sometime
Disorienting effect
Of the drug
Long way from sometime
Do with this
Do with this
Long way from sometime
Do with this
Dedicated or something
Long way from sometime
Do with this
Dedicated or something

On the take
Tendency toward self-pity
Dedicated or something
Tendency toward self-pity
Clean as a hound's tooth
Dedicated or something
On the take
Clean as a hound's tooth
Division division
Upstairs up here
Clean as a hound's tooth
Upstairs up here
Ain't sayin' who
Clean as a hound's tooth
Division division
Ain't sayin' who
Wrong answer
Fuckin' A right
Ain't sayin' who
Fuckin' A right
Got it analyzed
Ain't sayin who
Wrong answer
Got it analyzed
Tax-free
This one time
Got it analyzed

This one time
There was this crowd
Got it analyzed
Tax-free
There was this crowd
All these people
Behind that crowd
There was this crowd
Behind the crowd
Takin' the money
There was this crowd
All these people
Takin' the money
Not takin' the money
Confidential
Takin' the money
Confidential
Eyes and ears
Takin' the money
Not takin' the money
Eyes and ears
Sticky situation
Back to uniform
Eyes and ears
Back to uniform
What the
Eyes and ears

Sticky situation
What the
Not on
Told you straight
What the
Told you straight
Fuckin' word
What the
Not on
Fuckin' word
Somebody I know
Know what you're doin'
Fuckin' word
Know what you're doin'
Big deal friends
Fuckin' word
Somebody I know
Big deal friends
Head handed to me
Right on cue
Big deal friends
Right on cue
Ass on the line
Big deal friends
Head handed to me
Ass on the line
Out on me

Don't wanna
Ass on the line
Don't wanna
Come to bed
Ass on the line
Out on me
Come to bed
It's crossed my mind
Well do it
Come to bed
Well do it
Where's the drop
Come to bed
It's crossed my mind
Where's the drop
Got that
Record check
Where's the drop
Record check
Wash our own
Where's the drop
Got that
Wash our own
I'm splitting
Sit down
Wash our own
Sit down

Sit down
Wash our own
I'm splitting
Sit down
Owe you for that
Or should I
Sit down
Or should I
It's finished
Sit down
Owe you for that
It's finished
Cut the crap
Pick ups
It's finished
Pick ups
In case something should
It's finished
Cut the crap
In case something should
Happen to me
Out on a limb
In case something should
Out on a limb
Look
In case something should
Happen to me
Look

SUITE SIXTEEN

It takes two
times two

times two
times two, etc.

to be in
the company of

one

SHABBAT SALOON

The blue in the blueprint
Is the sensation of a concept

And the hue in the house
Is the concept of a sensation

No such thing
As a blue house

Any house of language
May appear opaque

On a transparent
Afternoon when

Linguists drop
Like duck phones

Tattoo blue
A grainy wonder

HEY NANCY

Meaning there will be a place to sit
Between the chair and thought of it

Have we arrived
And move

This time precludes
Light's lofty

Turn towards
The quotidian

But lichen a worm
In the beak to the

Bleak passage say
Take C to Kingston

Or the inversion
Susceptible to a tea

Take it that there is nothing
As pleasant as a pleasant day

Heron herring white moss on a wire
The pond becomes a lark

Slinks to a crawl
At either intersection

SHEDDING

for Thom

Which consonant
Becomes in time
The overtone of a bird
Tear at this veil
To kiss or cry
To see red or white
White or red
As the opposing tones
Of departure

To parse
Which consonant
From which to
Which from
Moment to
Moment departure
Is becoming
Another islet's
Inroad out

Leapt for fresh
Water compound
Becomes in time
A view

From a room
A room parsed
Aside as you pause
Please read
Aeration for air

The air that comes
Up for air and
Again goes under
The overtone of a bird
Cut off center
Circles the literal
Equator of the
Mind's reasons'
Holding pattern

And if you think
This is too fast
Try rereading
One phrase
Tear at this veil
At a time when
Bedeviling coevals
Ease into luke
Warm water together

Again when all else

Pales by comparison
Composition is a form
Of literary allusion
A makeshift blackbox
To kiss or cry
Shifts meaning over
To you the reader then
Gives you the shaft

In the opening field
When a literary executor
Pampers a palimpsest I
Love talking dirty
In opposing tones
I write to be read
To see red or white
From your prospective
Ovation betwixt us

Sound waves crash
Over water an audio
Mirage over water
Passes through holes
Where holes get
Out of Os
On their own
White or red

Sunspots in holes

In the quicksand
Of sense lunacy shivers
Down the backdrop
The veil behind every
Collection of white
Heat waves recollection
Spinning out
Constantly
As the opposing tones

Of departure
As the opposing tones
White or red
To see red or white
To kiss or cry
Tear at this veil
The overtone of a bird
Becomes in time
Which consonant

LINER NOTES

for Ulf

Life comes in
The middle
So let's mingle a
Little while

At the tattoo parlor
We were faking out
Soviet tanks
You'll never get

A better balloon than
This so why not knot
The question that
Inhales you

It don't matter
What you had or didn't
It's what you did
When it wasn't

Look at the sea
Running like Kraftwerk
I'm my own Sisyphus
In syrupy flavors

Or better yet tsunami
There's not a shred
Of decency left
So call a spade

A spade on
Speakerphone
Because wedding soup
Like a pink pup

On brown never
Tasted better

OR SAY A MARK

for Alan

Turning calligraphic
Sea frozen over
The event falls
Through itself

These tides this
Time each time
It could have been
Mind's lagoon

Spools out ligatures
Lift backward
Over the handlebars
Verbatim

Thinking of
Things in their absence
Working with things
As they are to play

Back this quote
Culled from form
As if memory were the kind of
Chase one could set aside

Mull over some
Time or another
To say it here again
The leading of

A phrase could
Change a life
When a splinter in
The real writes the readers'

Writer out of
And above each body
A shoulder
And each shoulder a beard

And each beard a face
And each face faces another
As the serif in
The surf's curl

Pulls back the
Sand at your feet

SQUARELY

Squarely arch
Tracks heist
Dreaming figures
A more pliable

Tomorrow again
Successions step
Carnations for
Plausible thaws

Forgetting disclosure
Stepping through
One tires of
Another

Someone else
Always here we do
Not know the water
With water

TREATISE

But beauty resembles what it
Cannot absorb the gill wilt

Faint light maneuvers
One sense or another

Coriander like a good soup ladles
Lentils love a cold war

Some hooligan's sneakers sucker
Punch the sidecar

Oasis doesn't detract from formal
Frontal intention

Along an excavation
A ballistic curve

No sleet shines like the present
The shivering shoe passes

Look before you leap but keep the
Creep out of my lap

The only access road I know is
Abscessed malignant encounters

Of the third kind

CARNATION

We hoist as we
Consider voilà
Windows glare
Delight stumbles

Through
Door strings
A perfect fourth
Drains corridor

Iridescent tolls
Just a road
In cursive
Parachutes fall

From sky
Goes white
Sun sums up
The afternoon

PICTURE DAY

Days inn arm left slept
Whilst others nix table
Spring centerfold all

In a glow they say
Mesquite down to
Wire and mean it
One hand washes

Afternoon over
Summer glances
Without language

Where would we be
Without thought
Where would we
Shimmer on wire

Meteors mess things
Up on all fours
Dog chases Q&A

See what I mean
By another name

Aren't you Diane
By another name

Who left whiskers
Got bail bond
Everyone happens

For a reason and so
On by another name
Shadows five-on-four
Spot me one flight
Up over symphony
You can hear it
For the devil day

After tomorrow
After September
Throw a slug in a
Cigarette machine

Sans fix time in slowmo
Pan to dusk out on
The runway what

You were saying
All goes gray
Verdict to deliver

Perfect strangers

Elaborate twist
No telling how it's
Gonna end (the

Convertible) while
The other hand
Returns to the scene
Of the poem

Early morning coffee
One thing leads to
Another remember

La Jolla you remember
La Jolla imagine all
The people sprocket
Holes in an afterlife

As if in a dream you
Can't be serious as if
In a dream suitcase in

Super 8 one whiff
Ergo sepia to believe
In something larger

Than a snooze bar

It was love alright
Fool with radio
San Diego waves

Wouldn't iota in the
Aftershave sparks
Knees make way for
Entropy off the books

I see neon sets the stage
During the war never
Heard from again

Ticker tape not a word
Of this on the roof
Just like that from
Whence rumor scatters

Up the coast soldiers
Get decorated
Everything resurfaces

Smile comes over you
Know my wallet in
Bed with nightcap

In the nick of

According to daughter
Business never been
Better in the hopper

Light snore lipstick
Off fifth deep down
Second to none by
Another name down

With degrees as if
The second person no
More no less credit's

Good till carpool
Tunnel cuts in a
Photo booth I can
See both ways

What should have
Been wind was
Seldom the face

Sublime in your
Season dayglo
Moon for miles

Around pin drops

Out goes road
On a cloud out goes
Or nothing at all

Coot on a whim
When will it be more
Than this the world's
An eve the grass is

3-D it looks better
Up close you nod
Off the more things

Change you know
How it is you know
How quarter spins
Lands on dime

Head's up hammock
Without a hitch some
Things add up

Other things don't
You fall out of touch
And I wonder
Where I stand

JUST PASSING THROUGH

Well it certainly has
Made me who I am
Today everything from
Being involved with
Occupy to going through
This injury has all made
Me who I am today and
I'm going I'm going
To use that in the
Future to effect even
More change and I
Look forward to
To being part of the
Ninety-nine percent
Here in 2012 to being
Part of IVAW here
In 2012 but I'm also maybe
Looking forward to
Returning to work part
Time and also maybe
Starting my old life
Again and see how
That goes for me

Author photo © Alasdair Schlesinger

Kyle Schlesinger is the author of a dozen books of poetry. He is proprietor of Cuneiform Press and Assistant Professor of Publishing at UHV.

About Chax Press

Chax Press is a 501(c)(3) nonprofit organization, founded in 1984, and has published more than 145 books, including fine art and trade editions of literature and book arts works.

For more information, please see our web site at http://chax.org

Chax Press is supported by individual contributions, and by the Tucson Pima Art Council and the Arizona Commision on the Arts, with funds from the State of Arizona and the National Endowment for the Arts.

TUCSON PIMA ARTS COUNCIL

Arizona Commission on the Arts

NATIONAL ENDOWMENT FOR THE ARTS